The Haitian Earthquake of 2010

PETER BENOIT

Children's Press®
An Imprint of Scholastic Inc.
New York   Toronto   London   Auckland   Sydney
Mexico City   New Delhi   Hong Kong
Danbury, Connecticut

Content Consultant
Solmaz Mohadjer
Director of Emergency Education Program
Teachers Without Borders

Library of Congress Cataloging-in-Publication Data

Benoit, Peter, 1955–
  The Haitian earthquake of 2010 / Peter Benoit.
    p. cm. — (A true book)
  Includes bibliographical references and index.
  ISBN-13: 978-0-531-25420-2 (lib. bdg.)   ISBN-13: 978-0-531-26625-0 (pbk.)
  ISBN-10: 0-531-25420-8 (lib. bdg.)   ISBN-10: 0-531-26625-7 (pbk.)
  1. Haiti Earthquake, Haiti, 2010—Juvenile literature. I. Title. II. Series.
  F1928.2.B46 2011
  972.94'073—dc22   2011007912

All rights reserved. Published in 2012 by Children's Press, an imprint of Scholastic Inc.
Printed in China 62
SCHOLASTIC, CHILDREN'S PRESS, A TRUE BOOK, and associated logos are trademarks and/or registered trademarks of Scholastic Inc.
1 2 3 4 5 6 7 8 9 10 R 21 20 19 18 17 16 15 14 13 12

Find the Truth!

Everything you are about to read is true *except* for one of the sentences on this page.

Which one is **TRUE**?

T or F   One year after the Haiti earthquake, no major reconstruction projects had begun.

T or F   The United States was the first country to come to the aid of Haiti after the quake.

Find the answers in this book.

Contents

THE BIG TRUTH!

Testing for cholera

Relief workers delivering water

4 Chaos!

What drove earthquake survivors to riot and loot? **31**

5 A Long Way to Go

What does the future hold for the people of Haiti? **39**

More than 20 nations sent aid to Haiti within three days of the earthquake.

About 95 percent of Haitians consider Creole their first language.

CHAPTER 1

Small Island, Big Earthquake

Haiti is a small nation on the island of Hispaniola in the Caribbean Sea, not far from the United States. Haiti shares Hispaniola with the Dominican Republic on the eastern side of the island. Haitians have two official languages: French and Creole. The French language was introduced by French settlers beginning in the 16th century. Creole is a mix of French and African languages, developed by enslaved Africans brought to the island by French and other European settlers.

A Haitian farmer walks along a canal, rebuilt with help from the United States to combat flooding.

Haiti comes from a native Arawak word meaning "mountainous land."

After years of fighting among European settlers, Africans, and mixed-heritage people, Haiti became an independent nation in 1804. In the years the followed, Haiti suffered continued unrest. By the 2000s, Haiti was one of the poorest nations in the world. An unstable government created problems in education, health care, and other government-run agencies. Food was also an issue. Most Haitians depended on small farms, but years of misuse had damaged the land and made farming difficult.

The earthquake affected people all across Haiti, not just in one area of the country.

Disaster Strikes

On January 12, 2010, the people of Léogâne, Haiti, were going about their business as usual. At 4:53 p.m., the ground began to shake violently. Six miles (9.7 kilometers) below the surface, two sides of a crack in the Earth's crust slid past each other a distance of up to 16 feet (4.9 meters). The shift released a powerful wave of destruction. Léogâne was located directly above the movement, at the earthquake's **epicenter**.

Some buildings crumbled as they were shaken off their **foundations**. Others not built well collapsed instantly and trapped thousands of Haitians under piles of rubble. Residents felt the shaking slow down after 35 seconds, but severe damage had been done. Roads were littered with the remains of destroyed homes and stores. Almost 90 percent of Léogâne's buildings were reduced to rubble. The few left standing were no longer safe to use.

After the earthquake, most roads were too cluttered by debris for cars to drive on them.

Before the earthquake, Léogâne's main industries were fishing and agriculture.

With so many buildings destroyed, the people of Léogâne lived in tents and other temporary shelters.

Waiting for Relief

Thousands of Léogâne's 134,000 inhabitants lost their lives. Most of the town was turned to dust. Survivors had to live in tents as they waited for help to arrive. The earthquake had left them without enough water to drink or food to eat. **Aftershocks** began soon after the earthquake ended. This made the situation even more disastrous.

The U.S. Navy and Canadian Forces reached Haiti about 10 days after the earthquake.

While aid workers did their best to arrive quickly, the severity of the earthquake made travel on the island very difficult.

Relief was slow to reach the people of Léogâne. Roads were too blocked for travel. The town's school and hospital were destroyed. It took five days for the first search and rescue teams from the United Kingdom and Iceland to reach the survivors. By then, more than 20,000 of the town's residents were dead. Many more were sick or wounded.

Trouble in the Capital

Léogâne was not the only town in Haiti to experience such horror. The same events occurred on an even larger scale in Port-au-Prince, Haiti's capital city, 18 miles (29 km) east of Léogâne. Port-au-Prince and its surrounding area had a population of almost two million before the quake. Tens of thousands died as buildings collapsed around them. The number of deaths couldn't be accurately counted because so many people had been killed.

The earthquake caused the most damage in Port-au-Prince because of the city's size.

The roof and towers of Port-au-Prince Cathedral collapsed. Only the walls were left standing. Government buildings were completely destroyed. The second floor of the National Palace, where the Haitian president lives, collapsed and fell onto the floor below. Thousands were injured and in need of medical attention, but the city's hospitals were in ruins. The main airport and seaport were both badly damaged. This made it difficult for **relief workers** to get into the city.

Many people needed immediate medical care.

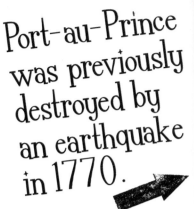

Port-au-Prince was previously destroyed by an earthquake in 1770.

Entire neighborhoods were reduced to rubble in Port-au-Prince.

A Nation Destroyed

The destruction swept throughout Haiti. Some authorities estimated that more than 300,000 Haitians had died. At least 50 hospitals and other health care buildings were destroyed. More than 1,300 schools were flattened. The destruction of radio stations and cell towers made it almost impossible to communicate. Life had changed forever for the earthquake survivors.

Huge crowds of people were forced to wait in line for food handouts.

In the first two months following the earthquake, the World Food Programme fed more than 2 million people.

CHAPTER 2

Coming to the Rescue

The destruction was enormous. Already poor and struggling, the country had to rely on the efforts of other nations. The neighboring Dominican Republic was the first nation to provide relief to Haiti. The Dominicans sent water and food. They also sent cooks and equipment to prepare the food. They made their airport available to receive aid from other countries. They sent surgeons, **trauma** specialists, and medical supplies. They even helped to restore some of Haiti's communication systems.

The World Joins In

Countries around the world quickly organized to join the tireless efforts of the Dominican rescue workers. Colombia sent rescue workers. Dozens of countries sent food, water, and **peacekeeping forces**. The United States sent food, water, and medical supplies. U.S. workers also opened roads leading to Port-au-Prince and surrounding towns. They also helped organize the many relief workers who had arrived in Haiti.

Soldiers helped keep order and distribute food supplies.

Rice and bottled water were among the basic necessities given to the earthquake victims.

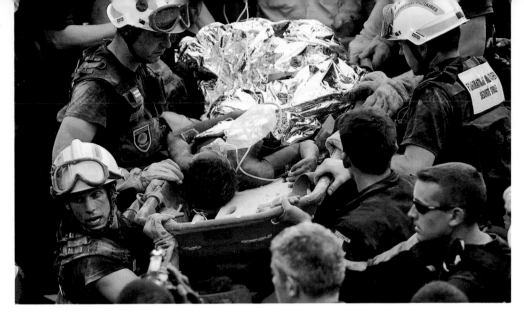

Some people were blocked inside destroyed buildings for weeks.

Trapped!

Rescue workers helped Haitians search through the rubble for missing family members and friends. There were occasional happy reunions as survivors were pulled from collapsed buildings. The Haitian government called off the official search after about 10 days. But some people were found alive even weeks after the earthquake. One man was trapped in a market for four weeks. Rescuers found him alive—but just barely.

The First Steps Toward Rebuilding

Helping Haiti to recover and rebuild would be very expensive. People around the world donated money to support the rebuilding efforts. The Interim Haiti Recovery Commission (IHRC) was established to decide how this money should be spent. Haitian prime minister Jean-Max Bellerive and former U.S. president Bill Clinton were named to head the commission. Even with so much help from other countries, the trouble in Haiti was far from over.

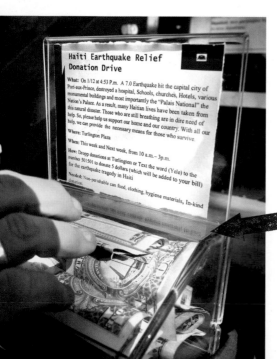

People around the world gave what they could to help the people of Haiti.

Haiti received less than half of the $2.8 billion in aid promised internationally in the year following the earthquake.

The Clinton Bush Haiti Fund

Haiti's poverty before the earthquake made recovery difficult. The country was not well organized and did not have the resources to help rebuild. Immediately after the earthquake hit, two former U.S. presidents joined forces to assist Haiti. Presidents Bill Clinton and George W. Bush started the Clinton Bush Haiti Fund to raise money. At first, all of the donations helped pay for the emergency workers and supplies needed to help survivors. Later, the fund was used to create new jobs and businesses for Haitians. Dozens of other organizations also continued to help Haiti in its time of need.

How Strong Was It?

Thousands of earthquakes occur every year. Scientists measure their strength using a system known as the Moment Magnitude Scale (MMS). The system assigns each earthquake a number based on its power. The earthquake in Haiti measured 7.0 on the MMS. Few earthquakes measure above 6.0, and very few have ever been recorded above 9.0. Most fall between 3.0 and 4.0 and are hardly noticed by people.

China:
May 12, 2008

An earthquake with a magnitude of 7.9 destroyed about 80 percent of the buildings in the towns and cities near the epicenter of the earthquake in Sichuan Province in China. About 90,000 people were killed, and millions lost their homes.

Chile:
February 27, 2010

Weeks after the Haiti earthquake, a major earthquake occurred in Chile. It measured 8.8 in magnitude but fewer people died than in Haiti. Chile had learned from its history of earthquakes and was better prepared.

Japan:
March 11, 2011

A massive earthquake with a magnitude of 9.0 occurred off the east coast of Japan. The earthquake caused gigantic tsunami waves to flood parts of the country. It was one of the five most powerful earthquakes ever recorded.

The cholera outbreak caused the situation in Haiti to become even worse.

CHAPTER 3

Adding Insult to Injury

Relief efforts continued in the months following the earthquake. But in October, Haiti was hit with yet another disaster. People began to get very sick. On October 21, 2010, authorities said that Haiti was experiencing an outbreak of cholera, a bacterial infection that causes severe diarrhea and vomiting. Cholera is usually from **contaminated** food or water. The disease can be treated with medicine, but it can quickly kill if medicine is not available.

Haiti had not experienced a cholera outbreak in more than 50 years.

The Nepalese base was guarded to prevent protesters from getting too close and possibly harming the force.

Blame Game

Scientists were able to trace the outbreak's origin to Haiti's Atribonite River. The strain, or kind, of cholera they found is usually found in east Asian countries. Because peacekeeping forces from the east Asian country of Nepal were camped along the river, many blamed them for the outbreak. Protesters called for the Nepalese peacekeepers to leave immediately. However, the Nepalese denied the accusation and no proof was found that they were the cause. The cause remains unknown.

A New Goal

Sick people needed medicine and medical care. The disease was spreading faster in Haiti than it would have spread in other countries. Haiti is small, but it has a large population of more than nine million people. Because Haiti is so poor, Haitians often lack fresh water and soap to keep themselves clean and healthy. Relief groups began sending soap and water-cleaning chemicals. But it was not enough to control the cholera outbreak.

Many Haitians were given water purifiers to help prevent the disease from spreading.

A single water purifier can provide about 4,700 gallons of clean water.

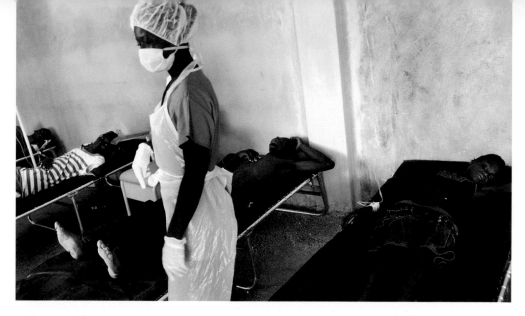

Makeshift clinics were set up to treat the cholera victims.

The Disease Spreads

The disease continued to spread. By the end of October, more than 4,000 cases of cholera were reported in Haiti. The disease made its way to the neighboring Dominican Republic. By the end of 2010, more than 140,000 people had fallen sick, and more than 80,000 had been hospitalized. Estimates put the death toll from cholera at more than 3,000. Every province of Haiti reported cases of cholera. The situation had grown into a full **epidemic**.

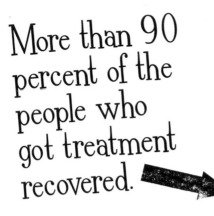

More than 90 percent of the people who got treatment recovered.

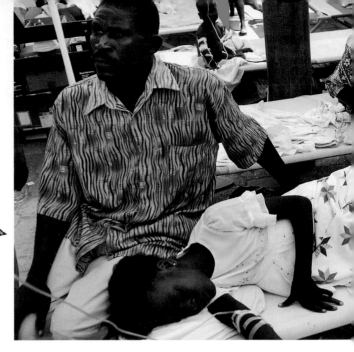

Because there were not enough medical workers, many cholera patients had to wait a long time for treatment.

By early 2011, cholera had spread as far as Venezuela in South America. More than 20 Venezuelans returned home with cholera symptoms after visiting the Dominican Republic. Rescue workers in Haiti did their best to treat the outbreak. But many health facilities were already full. Sick people lined the hallways in hospitals. Relief workers set up tents in open areas such as parking lots. Haitians were still angry about the outbreak.

Some people collected bricks and other building materials from destroyed buildings.

CHAPTER 4

Chaos!

The people of Haiti were frustrated. They had experienced two major disasters in less than a year. Some Haitians blamed relief workers for making the situation worse. Others became desperate to get supplies and medicine for their families. Many Haitians began rioting and **looting**. They attacked relief workers, started fires, and stole supplies. The situation grew more dangerous every day.

Stores in Port-au-Prince's main shopping areas were emptied by looters.

Frustrated Haitians resorted to violent protests to express their anger.

Enough Is Enough

Many Haitians were upset that the Nepalese workers were not being punished or sent back home. Some Haitian protesters became violent. They threw rocks and bottles at United Nations peacekeepers. They also built walls of tires and set them on fire to block roadways used by relief workers.

As days passed, the protests grew deadly. On November 16, a police station in the town of Cap-Haitien was set on fire. Protesters also looted a warehouse filled with food donations and then set it on fire. Some protesters fired guns at peacekeeping soldiers, forcing the troops to fire back. At least one protester was killed. Haitian president René Préval asked for an end to the violence. Extra soldiers were called in to prevent more attacks.

René Préval was first elected president of Haiti in 1995.

Préval's words did little to discourage the protests.

Many Haitians did not want foreign soldiers in their country.

Why Are They Here?

Hundreds of peacekeeping troops were staying in Haiti to help keep order in the troubled country. But their presence began to anger many Haitians. Many Haitians believed that they would be better off if the peacekeeping troops were gone. It was expensive to house and feed the forces. Haitian protesters believed that this money could be better spent rebuilding Haiti's own police forces and courts. Some relief workers agreed.

Supply Problems

The violence took a toll on Haiti's food and medical supplies. "The food you are pillaging [looting] belongs to schoolchildren, sick people in hospitals, the poor," said President Préval. The violence also prevented new supplies from arriving. The United Nations and other organizations canceled flights of supply planes to Haiti. The World Health Organization stopped training medical relief workers. These organizations did not want their workers to get injured in Haiti.

People swarmed supply trucks to avoid waiting in line for rations.

Election Trouble

Haiti's presidential election was held in November 2010. President Préval could not run because he had already served two terms. He encouraged Haitians to vote for Jude Célestin. But many Haitians believed that Préval had dealt with the disaster poorly and wouldn't support his candidate. They supported candidates such as Mirlande Manigat and popular singer Michel Martelly. Haitians hoped one of these new candidates would lead the country to recovery.

The First Year After the Earthquake

January 12, 2010

A massive earthquake hits Haiti.

March

Donors pledge $9.9 billion to the IHRC to help rebuild Haiti.

Haiti Earthquake Relief Donation Drive

In Haiti, a candidate needs 50 percent of the vote to win. Manigat received the most votes, at 31.4 percent. Martelly was second, with 21.8 percent. No one received enough votes to become president. In addition, many Haitians believed there had been cheating. Violent protests broke out. In March 2011, another election was held between the top two candidates, Manigat and Martelly. Martelly won nearly 70 percent of the vote. In April, he became Haiti's new president.

October 21
Authorities report a cholera outbreak.

November
Haiti's presidential election is held.

January 2011
No major reconstruction projects have begun.

Workers have helped to clean some of the debris, but new construction has yet to begin.

CHAPTER 5

A Long Way to Go

More than one year after the quake struck, Haiti was still suffering. No major construction projects had been started. Many of Haiti's buildings still were in ruins. People continued to live in tents and makeshift shelters. Cholera also continued to be a problem. Thousands of people were living without electricity or clean water. Hundreds of thousands had no jobs.

A year after the earthquake about 800,000 Haitians were still living in temporary shelters.

Frustrated at long food lines after the earthquake, some resorted to stealing food.

Why Is It Taking So Long?

Authorities cannot agree on the cause of Haiti's continued problems. Some blame looters and rioters who disrupted relief efforts and harmed peaceful survivors. Unfortunately, peacekeeping forces and Haitian police are sometimes overwhelmed and unable to prevent crime. Other people believe that the world has turned its back on Haiti. Some Haitian leaders have spoken out against the international community for its failure to help.

A Plan for the Future

On December 14, 2010, the IHRC created a list of seven important goals it wants to achieve. The goals are to make improvements in housing, debris removal, education, energy, health, job creation, and water and **sanitation**. For example, the IHRC plans to create proper housing for at least 400,000 people and train 5,000 new teachers. The organization has estimated the cost of each goal to make sure it fits into its budget. If the plan succeeds, it will put Haiti on the path to a full recovery.

What's Next for Haiti?

Haiti's reconstruction will be a long and difficult process. Some experts predict that it could take decades. In Port-au-Prince alone, the United Nations estimates that three-quarters of the city needs to be rebuilt. Haitian recovery will require hard work and a great deal of money. It will also need strong leadership. Only time will tell what the future holds for Haiti. ★

Workers continue the massive task of clearing rubble and destroyed buildings.

Haitian people were paid by relief organizations to help clear debris.

Measurement of the 2010 Haiti earthquake on the Moment Magnitude Scale: 7.0

Number of people who died in the first days after the earthquake: Up to 300,000

Number of people living in tents a year after the earthquake: About 800,000

Number of people who caught cholera by the end of 2010: At least 140,000

Number of people who died due to cholera by the end of 2010: More than 3,000

Amount of money pledged to Haiti's recovery by IHRC donors: $9.9 billion

Did you find the truth?

T One year after the Haiti earthquake, no major reconstruction projects had begun.

F The United States was the first country to come to the aid of Haiti after the quake.

Resources

Books

Aronin, Miriam. *Earthquake in Haiti*. New York: Bearport Publishing, 2011.

Yomtov, Nel. *Haiti*. New York: Children's Press, 2012.

Lies, Anne. *The Earthquake in Haiti*. Edina, MN: ABDO Publishing, 2011.

Prokos, Anna. *Earthquakes*. Pleasantville, NY: Gareth Stevens, 2009.

Spilsbury, Louise, and Richard Spilsbury. *Shattering Earthquakes*. Chicago: Heinemann Library, 2010.

Than, Ker. *Earthquakes*. New York: Children's Press, 2009.

Organizations and Web Sites

Embassy of Haiti, Washington, D.C.

www.haiti.org

Find a wealth of information on Haiti as well as on the services offered by the embassy.

New York Times—Haiti

www.nytimes.com/info/haiti-earthquake-2010

Read the full story of the earthquake, including details about relief efforts, the Haitian government's response, and how to help.

Oxfam—Haiti Earthquake

www.oxfam.org.uk/oxfam_in_action/emergencies/haiti-earthquake.html

Learn what this international relief organization is doing to help Haiti, and read about its work in other places around the world.

UN News Centre—News Focus: Haiti

www.un.org/apps/news/infocusRel.asp?infocusID=91&Body=Haiti&Body1=

Get the latest updates on the situation in Haiti through reports, articles, and videos.

USAID/Haiti: Post-Earthquake Response

www.usaid.gov/ht/helphaiti.html

Learn how this organization is aiding Haiti through economic recovery, food assistance, education, health, and shelter.

Important Words

aftershocks (AF-tur-shahkz)—smaller earthquakes that occur after an earthquake, in the same area

contaminated (kun-TAM-ih-nay-ted)—containing harmful substances, such as disease-causing bacteria

epicenter (EP-i-sen-tur)—location at the surface of the Earth directly above where an earthquake occurs or originates

epidemic (ep-i-DEM-ik)—an infectious disease that makes a large number of people sick at the same time

foundations (foun-DAY-shuhnz)—solid structures on which buildings are constructed

looting (LOO-ting)—stealing from shops or homes during a riot, war, natural disaster, or other crisis

magnitude (MAG-ni-tood)—a measurement of the severity of an earthquake

peacekeeping forces (PEES-kee-ping FORC-ez)—soldiers trained to keep order in places where there is unrest

relief workers (ri-LEEF WUR-kurz)—people who help others recover from an accident

sanitation (san-i-TAY-shuhn)—systems for cleaning the water supply and disposing of sewage and garbage

trauma (TRAW-muh)—severe physical or emotional pain

Index

Page numbers in **bold** indicate illustrations

About the Author

Peter Benoit is educated as a mathematician but has many other interests. He has taught and tutored high school and college students for many years, mostly in math and science. He also runs summer workshops for writers and students of literature. Mr. Benoit has also written more than 2,000 poems. His life has been one committed to learning. He lives in Greenwich, New York.

PHOTOGRAPHS © 2012: AP Images: 19 (Gregory Bull), 40 (Ariana Cubillos), 41 (Manuel Diaz), cover, 26 (Ramon Espinosa), 20, 36 right, 43 (Doug Finger/The Gainesville Sun), 23 center (Juan Gonzalez), 32 (Emilio Morenatti), 9 (Ryan Remiorz/The Canadian Press), 21 (Jorge Saenz), 23 bottom (Hou Yu/Color China Photo); Clifford Oliver Photography/www.cliffordoliverphotography.com: 48; Corbis Images: 16 (Niko Guido), back cover, 27 (Adam Stoltman); Getty Images: 5 bottom (Win McNamee), 12 (Erin Oberholtzer/U.S. Navy), 11 (Alison Wright/National Geographic); Jim McMahon: 6; Landov, LLC/Reuters: 38 (Kena Betancur), 23 top (David Gray), 5 top, 35 (Tatyana Makeyeva), 30 (Eduardo Munoz), 14 (Shannon Stapleton); NEWSCOM: 33 (Orlando Barria/EFE), 10 (Thomas Coex/AFP/Getty Images), 34 (imago stock&people), 42 (Emily Troutman/AFP/Getty Images); Panos Pictures/Jeroen Oerlemans: 22, 23 background; Redux Pictures: 28, 29, 37 left (Michael Appleton/The New York Times), 37 right (Julie Platner); Scholastic Library Publishing, Inc.: 44; U.S. Navy Photo/Senior Chief Mass Communication Specialist Spike Call: 18; USAID/Jean-Charles Herve: 8; VII Photo Agency LLC/Ron Haviv: 3, 4, 13, 15, 24, 36 left.